OUR
QUEEN

OUR QUEEN

Elizabeth II : A Celebration of Her Majesty's Friendship with the People of Canada

Editor: Patti Tasko
Photo Editor: Ron Poling

THE CANADIAN PRESS

WILEY

John Wiley & Sons Canada, Ltd.

Library and Archives Canada Cataloguing in Publication Data

Our queen : Elizabeth II : a celebration of Her Majesty's friendship with the people of Canada / the Canadian Press; Patti Tasko, editor; Ron Poling, photo editor.

ISBN 978-0-470-15444-1

    1. Elizabeth II, Queen of Great Britain, 1926- —Pictorial works. 2. Elizabeth II, Queen of Great Britain, 1926- —Travel—Canada—Pictorial works. 3. Elizabeth II, Queen of Great Britain, 1926-. 4. Elizabeth II, Queen of Great Britain, 1926- —Travel—Canada. I. Canadian Press II. Tasko, Patti III. Poling, Ron IV. Title.

DA590.O97 2007   941.085'092   C2007-905550-8

Production Credits
Cover and interior design: Adrian So
Back cover photo: Jonathan Hayward
Printer: Friesens

John Wiley & Sons Canada, Ltd.
6045 Freemont Blvd.
Mississauga, Ontario
L5R 4J3

Printed in Canada

This book is printed with biodegradable vegetable-based inks.

1 2 3 4 5 FP 11 10 09 08 07

THE CANADIAN PRESS

Jeff McIntosh/The Canadian Press

Dear Reader,

This publication is a collection of our most prized images. Some of the images you may have seen before in your local newspaper. Others you may be seeing for the first time.

High-quality prints of many of the photographs in this book may be purchased for personal use.

For information about acquiring images from The Canadian Press, please visit us at http://www.thecanadianpress.com; call 1-866-599-0599; or email us at archives@cpimages.com

CONTENTS

INTRODUCTION

John Ulan/The Canadian Press

CHAPTER 1

Chuck Stoody/The Canadian Press

AMONG CANADIAN ICONS

CHAPTER 2

Kevin Frayer/The Canadian Press

THE CANADIAN ARMED FORCES

CHAPTER 3

CANADA'S FIRST NATIONS

www.cpimages.com

CHAPTER 4

HORSES AND HOUNDS

90

CHAPTER 5

THE QUEEN AND HER MINISTERS

108

CHAPTER 6

THE QUEEN'S FAMILY IN CANADA

CHAPTER 7

Paul Chiasson/The Canadian Press

THE ELEMENTS

182

CHAPTER 8

Andrew Vaughan/The Canadian Press

HER HATS

198

CHAPTER 9

Max Nash/The Associated Press

ROYAL TOURS FROM
BEHIND THE LENS

214

CHAPTER 10

Ron Poling/The Canadian Press

MILESTONES IN A
ROYAL LIFE

232

INTRODUCTION

www.cpimages.com

∧ The Queen reads newspapers on the Concorde during her flight home after her Silver Jubilee tour of Canada and the West Indies, 1977.

< Princess Elizabeth in *Aladdin* pantomime, December 1943.

Horse-crazy little girl. Glamorous young princess. Solemn monarch. Smiling grandmother. The many faces of Queen Elizabeth II are intertwined with the Canadian identity.

She was only 10 years old when her photograph first appeared on a Canadian postage stamp, and since then Queen Elizabeth II has been photographed in every nook and cranny of the country. The Queen has been present for most significant Canadian events of the past 50 years. She gave us our flag and Constitution, helped us celebrate birthdays and anniversaries, and her name can be seen on hundreds of roads, hospitals, parks, theatres, schools, and even a power station.

She is the face of the monarchy and most Canadians don't even remember who came before her. Yet Elizabeth ended up as Queen of the United Kingdom, Canada, and the Commonwealth as much by a twist of fate as by the grace of God.

The daughter and granddaughter of men who themselves were not first in line to the throne, Elizabeth should have lived and died in relative regal obscurity. Instead, she became one of the world's most famous women at the age of 25, when her

Aaron Harris/The Canadian Press

∧ The Queen tours CBC offices in Toronto in October 2002.

Jeff McIntosh/The Canadian Press

< A girl catches the Queen on a camera phone as she tours Saskatoon to help Saskatchewan celebrate its 100th birthday.

The Queen and Right Rev. Victoria Matthews, Bishop of Edmonton, leave St. Mary and St. George Anglican Church in Jasper, Alberta, in May 2005.

father's premature death in 1952, made her England's sixth ruling queen.

Elizabeth's father, King George VI, was a second son and not expected to reach the throne. However, in 1936, his older brother, King Edward VIII, announced his unexpected abdication, giving up his throne "for the woman I love"—Wallis Warfield Simpson, an American divorcee.

Elizabeth Alexandra Mary Windsor had been born 10 years earlier, on April 21, 1926, and christened with the names of three queens—her mother, grandmother, and great-grandmother.

She passed her early years in an intimate family atmosphere free from any hint of future royal responsibilities.

When she was four, her sister Margaret Rose was born. The two girls frolicked happily together, Elizabeth's seriousness and sense of appropriateness an engaging contrast to Margaret's ingrained mischievousness.

The abdication of her uncle changed the family intimacy and the years of being watched closely began for the future queen. The new King, his wife Elizabeth, and their two daughters were a popular symbol of a happy, close-knit family with a British public made weary by first the Depression, then the trials of the Second World War.

Elizabeth's 1947 marriage to Lieutenant Philip Mountbatten, a dashing young sailor, provided a splash of colour in a time of drab austerity. There were conflicting stories about how the two met, but there was no conflict over the fact that it was a love match. Marion Crawford, Elizabeth's governess for 17 years, claims that the young princess was 13 at the first meeting and that she was most impressed by the 18-year-old Philip's capacity for tucking away plates of shrimp.

On November 14, 1948, six days before the first anniversary of the royal wedding, Charles, the future Prince of Wales and heir to the throne, was born. He was followed by three more children—Princess Anne in 1950, Prince Andrew in 1960, and Prince Edward in 1964.

When her father, a heavy smoker who developed lung cancer, died unexpectedly on February 6, 1952, Elizabeth and Philip were 6,500 kilometres away in the African jungle, on the

^ Prime Minister Pierre Trudeau, the Queen, and Prince Philip in the Senate chambers in 1977.

< The Queen pays tribute to Alberta's pioneers during an address to the provincial legislature in May 2005. It was the first speech to the legislature by a reigning monarch.

first leg of what was to have been a five-month tour. It was the first time in the history of the Commonwealth that a sovereign acceded to the throne while abroad.

In her declaration of accession at St. James Palace, Queen Elizabeth II said: "My heart is too full for me to say more to you today than that I shall always work . . . to uphold constitutional government and to advance the happiness and prosperity of my people, spread as they are all the world over."

Canada was the first Commonwealth country to proclaim her as Queen Elizabeth II. The title Queen of Canada came a year later, in 1953, by an act of Parliament in Ottawa. The

∧ The Queen and Prime Minister Jean Chrétien leave the stage following Canada Day ceremonies in Ottawa in 1997.

< Princess Elizabeth trains as an officer in the Auxiliary Transport Service in April 1945. The ATS was established by the Women's Auxiliary Army Corps during the Second World War.

Queen was officially declared head of state, though all her powers and authority were delegated to the Governor General.

To allow for a period of mourning for the King, the pomp and pageantry of Coronation Day wasn't held until June 2, 1953. Six kings and seven queens attended as Elizabeth rode to Westminster Abbey in a gilded coach and dedicated herself to her people in the world's oldest state ceremonial. It was the most-watched coronation in history. Only a few hundred could crowd into the ancient abbey, but millions watched on television and a colour motion picture film was shown around the world.

The Queen ascended to the throne at the onset of the nuclear age, when a Cold War disturbed relations between East and West. In Britain, a quiet social and economic revolution was taking place. In the Commonwealth, new nations were seeking greater self-determination in growing numbers. In Canada, post-war immigrants were continuing to pour in and the country was becoming decidedly less English in its culture and traditions.

Elizabeth, ever her father's daughter, took her role as Queen seriously. For Canada, this meant an unprecedented number of visits.

She was present for seven of Canada's birthdays and celebrated many provincial centennials and anniversaries. She opened the St. Lawrence Seaway in 1959, toured Expo 67, attended the 1976 Montreal Olympics and the 1978 Commonwealth Games in Edmonton and the 1994 Commonwealth Games in Victoria, and visited on both her silver and golden jubilees. In 1982, Queen Elizabeth II was in Ottawa for one of Canada's proudest moments as a nation, when, with her signature, the Canadian Constitution was proclaimed.

The major royal visits in the 1950s caused huge excitement. Every little detail was treated as important news. "Princess Bringing Crinolines" was one *Globe and Mail* headline before the 1951 royal visit.

"The Queen and Philip, in those days, were the magic that Charles and Diana became in their early relationship," Canadian Press journalist Bruce Levett, who covered the Ontario and Quebec leg of a coast-to-coast 1959 tour, once said. "I can't recall a single anti-royal incident. Mainly, I remember the small towns with the people cheering and waving flags as the train pulled slowly through."

Chuck Mitchell/The Canadian Press

^ The Queen, with Prime Minister Brian Mulroney, cuts into a giant birthday cake at July 1 celebrations in Ottawa in 1992.

Hayes/The Canadian Press

∧ The Queen and Prince Philip arrive for the opening
ceremonies of the 1976 Olympics in Montreal on
July 17, 1976.

The tours often had a repetitive similarity and perhaps this is why media focused on such inconsequential details. Even this repetitiveness became the topic of controversy. On the eve of the 1959 visit, *Weekend Magazine* ran an article titled "Let's End Cruelty to Royalty" which criticized royal tours for being pointless and fatiguing, a series of endless reviews of honour guards and handshaking with politicians but with no actual meetings with any "Canadians at large."

The handshaking alone must have been exhausting. During a 10-day visit in 1957, the Queen and Prince Philip greeted, individually, 10,000 people.

When the Queen visited Canada during the 1967 Centennial, an attempt was made to shake up the royal tour format and come up with something fresher for the swinging '60s. The tour script was rewritten to include mass gatherings with what, at the time, were described by a Canadian Press reporter as "mod touches." These included a six-metre-tall birthday cake for Canada on Parliament Hill, sliced by the Queen, and a rock 'n' roll band. Trumpeter Bobby Gimby played his hit tune *Ca-na-da* and it was followed by the release of balloons and a 100-gun salute.

In 1970, radio reports from the Queen's visit were broadcast live from Resolute Bay, 1,770 kilometres above the North Pole.

The 1984 royal visit was unusual as it spanned three prime ministers from preparation to execution: it was prepared by Prime Minister Pierre Trudeau, was postponed by Prime Minister John Turner so an election could be held, and took place after Prime Minister Brian Mulroney, who won the election, took office.

In 2005, the 79-year-old Queen earned admiration for stoically battling cold, driving rain as she toured Alberta and Saskatchewan to mark their centennials. Canadian Press reporter Michelle MacAfee expected that public interest in the trip would be limited, especially among younger generations. "But I found quite the opposite to be true," says MacAfee.

∧ The Queen walks about the international zone of the athletes' village at the Commonwealth Games in Victoria in 1994. She chatted with athletes, coaches, and volunteers.

"She drew large crowds everywhere she went, young and old, from all cultures, and those lucky enough to be treated to some polite chit-chat had the same kind of afterglow others reserve for encounters with movie stars or pro athletes."

Most of the tours were met with enthusiasm. One notable exception was a 1964 visit to Quebec City to mark the centenary of the 1864 talks that led to Confederation. The visit, designed to celebrate the unification of the country, ended up bringing attention to the secession movement in Quebec and seemed to highlight a widening in the gulf between French- and English-speaking Canada.

Separatists threatened the Queen's life and told her to stay home. After much discussion on whether the trip should be cancelled, it went ahead. "Queen flies to Canada; Britons pray for safety," read one newspaper headline.

She was greeted by a few hundred protesters in Quebec City amid very tight security that later led to a riot after municipal police armed with batons charged the crowd, terrifying and injuring bystanders as well as protesters. Police action was denounced by many as excessive and brought comparisons to civil rights clashes in American cities.

Back in England, she was greeted by 1,000 spectators at the airport after a newspaper appealed to Londoners to show their praise for a woman who "showed true courage in going to Canada at this difficult time."

There have been a few other controversial visits among the dozens the Queen has made to Canada. In 1990, her Canada Day visit to Ottawa and neighbouring Hull, now Gatineau, Quebec, was seen by some as an insult to Quebec.

The visit had been timed to celebrate the ratification of the Meech Lake accord, which was meant to answer many of Quebec's constitutional concerns. But the accord officially died a few days before her visit to the capital. Although pro-sovereigntist sentiment within Quebec was running high, the Queen's visit continued as planned, without violence. "Knowing Canadians as well as I do," she said, "I cannot believe that they will not be able, after a period of calm reflection, to find a way through present difficulties."

During her 2002 Golden Jubilee visit, Queen Elizabeth II had to run a gauntlet of angry protestors outside a state dinner at the Canadian Museum of Civilization, again in Gatineau, Quebec. The group of about 50 demonstrators carried Quebec fleur-de-lys flags and chanted "We want a country, not a monarchy" and "Queen go home."

During the Queen's reign, Canada lost much of its British culture, thanks to the twin factors of diverse immigration and American cultural influences. It started during the Trudeau years, when the Queen's likeness was dropped from many stamps and bank notes, the letters HM disappeared from government documents, and O Canada replaced God Save the Queen.

In the 1990s, the monarchy was embarrassed by the antics of the Queen's children. Salacious tabloid headlines focused on the divorces of Charles, Andrew, and Anne, often under messy circumstances. Tapes and private conversations surfaced that put some members of the Royal Family in a less than favourable light.

But never the Queen herself, even when she was deliberately tricked. In 1995, a Montreal radio host got her on the phone

∧ The Queen at Upper Canada Village in Morrisburg, Ontario, in 1976.

∧ The Queen leaves the airport in Victoria during her Golden Jubilee tour of Canada in October 2002.

by pretending to be Prime Minister Jean Chrétien. Raymond Brassard, a jokester notorious for luring unsuspecting celebrities into interviews, chatted on-air with the Queen for 17 minutes. Although he managed to get her to delve into the sensitive political area of Quebec separatism—something she would normally avoid in public—she said nothing embarrassing. In reference to the upcoming referendum on Quebec's status, the Queen said she was following the campaign and "If I can help in any way, I will be very happy to do so."

About the only mistake the Queen has made came after the death of her former daughter-in-law, Diana, in 1997. The Royal Family were on holidays at Balmoral Castle in Scotland when the news broke and the Queen did not immediately return to London, preferring to stay in the "quiet haven" of Scotland to grieve with her grandsons, said a spokesperson.

Buckingham Palace remained shuttered and, because the Queen was not there, according to the rules of protocol, no flag flew at half-mast. "Where is our Queen? Where is her flag?" asked a headline in *The Sun*. "Your people are suffering. Speak to us, Ma'am," instructed *The Mirror*. The Queen did finally return to London, made a statement on TV, and ordered that, in defiance of protocol, a Union Jack be flown at half-mast from the flagpole at the palace. For many, the Queen's delayed reaction showed how out of touch she was with a modern public.

At a luncheon a few months later to mark her 50th wedding anniversary, the Queen indicated that the Royal Family had learned from its mistakes. Noting that a hereditary monarchy only exists "with the support and consent of the people," she acknowledged that was sometimes difficult for an institution so steeped in tradition. "For us … the message is often harder to read, obscured as it can be by deference, rhetoric or the conflicting currents of public opinion. But read it we must," she said.

By 2002, the monarchy witnessed something of a revival as Elizabeth marked her Golden Jubilee, becoming only the fifth British monarch to reign for 50 years. It was a year that began in sadness, first with the death of her sister, Margaret, followed less than two months later by the death of her mother. The losses seemed to inspire a sympathetic fondness for the Royal

Tim Clark/The Canadian Press

∧ The Queen, wearing her coronation gown, and
Prince Philip, in the uniform of a colonel-in-chief
of the Royal Canadian Regiment, ride in an open
carriage to open Canada's Parliament on October
14, 1957.

< Prince Philip kisses his wife goodbye at Sudbury
Airport in 1984.

Family. The jubilee celebrations ended with a trip to Canada where she dropped a puck at a National Hockey League game. It was a remarkable change from the usual type of royal events, showing Canadians the Queen understood their interests and could be a good sport.

That image, and many others of the Queen throughout the years, have been gathered in the pages of this book. Canadian Press photographers have trailed the Queen on every one of her Canadian tours, by train, plane, car, ship, and even dogsled. These are the most memorable photographs from the thousands taken during visits that have made Elizabeth Canada's Queen in more than name.

—by Patti Tasko with files from Kevin Ward

Jacques Boissinot/The Canadian Press

∧ Arthur Maxwell House, lieutenant-governor of Newfoundland and Labrador, watches the Queen plant a tree in St. John's in 1997.

> The Queen accepts flowers as she leaves the Alberta legislature in Edmonton in 2005.

> Accompanied by assembly Speaker Kevin O'Brien, the Queen looks at a stone sculpture in Iqaluit that commemorates the dedication of the legislative assembly of Nunavut. It was the first day of her 2002 Golden Jubilee tour of Canada.

< Ottawa on the morning of October 13, 1957 as the Queen and Prince Philip place a wreath at the Canadian War Memorial. The building at right is the Chateau Laurier.

Paul Chiasson/The Canadian Press

CHAPTER 1
AMONG CANADIAN ICONS

Throughout six decades, the Queen has visited nearly all significant Canadian landmarks and attended many of the country's major birthday and anniversary celebrations. She has been photographed with many of our official symbols, such as the beaver and the Maple Leaf flag.

But the event that has been, arguably, the most "Canadian" in royal history came during her Golden Jubilee visit to Vancouver in 2002, when the Queen strode onto centre ice with the monarch of hockey, Wayne Gretzky, and dropped the puck at a National Hockey League game.

As spectators at the packed pre-season game cheered wildly with approval, Gretzky handed the puck to the Queen, who

displayed what some would call a rookie technique, crouching slightly at the knees and gingerly dropping the puck.

The Queen and Gretzky were also accompanied onto the ice by former hockey great Howie Meeker, Vancouver Canucks defenceman Ed Jovanovski, and Cassie Campbell, captain of the Canadian women's Olympic gold medal team.

The Queen sat with Gretzky and British Columbia Premier Gordon Campbell during the first period. "She was curious

˄ The Queen and Prince Philip attend a Canadian Football League game at Ottawa's Lansdowne Park in 1979. Also shown are Gerry Organ of the Ottawa Rough Riders (right) and Terry Evenshen of the Hamilton Tiger Cats (centre, right.) Both Organ and Evenshen were the senior Canadian players on their teams and both were born in England.

> Wayne Gretzky escorts the Queen to centre ice so she can drop the puck at a ceremonial faceoff at GM Place in Vancouver on October 6, 2002.

about why penalties were being called," Gretzky later told reporters. "She also talked about the goaltenders and how quick they were."

It was an event many would have never thought possible: a monarch paying tribute to Canada's favourite sport with such a substantial gesture. The event overshadowed everything else

< The Queen greets a crowd gathered outside St. Mary and St. George Anglican Church in Jasper, Alberta in 2005. Whistler Mountain is in the background.

^ David Alan-Williams, captain of the *Matthew*, flanked by Prince Philip (left), the Queen, and Brian Tobin, premier of Newfoundland and Labrador, shows off the vessel at dockside in Bonavista, Newfoundland, in 1997. The voyage from Bristol, England celebrated the 500th anniversary of John Cabot's arrival in North America.

on the carefully planned tour. "I've dealt with more interest in this puck dropping than anything in my career," said John Anderson, media co-ordinator for the royal tour.

It wasn't the first time the Queen had attended a Canadian hockey game, however. In 1951, as a 25-year-old princess, Elizabeth watched one period of play between the Toronto Maple Leafs and Chicago Blackhawks during her first visit to Canada. Later the same day in Montreal, the royal couple

> The Queen meets admirers in Jasper, Alberta, in 2005.

Andrew Vaughan/The Canadian Press

Paul Chiasson/The Canadian Press

Frank Gunn/The Canadian Press

Paul Chiasson/The Canadian Press

< A town crier reads a proclamation to the Queen at a festival in Toronto in 2002.

∧ The Queen delivers a speech from the throne at the Nunavut legislative assembly in Iqaluit on October 4, 2002.

watched another game between the Canadiens and New York Rangers.

The Queen has seen more of the country than most Canadians. Her expansive travels have extended from the Far North to the southernmost tip of Ontario, and from where John Cabot landed on Newfoundland's east coast to Tofino on the west coast of Vancouver Island. Of course, many of these trips have been by train, an icon that symbolizes the building of the Canadian nation.

The Queen has become intimately familiar with many other icons and images associated with Canada. Her travels have included historically significant sites such as Parliament Hill and each of Canada's ten provincial legislatures; geographic

∧ Singer Buffy Sainte-Marie and members of her band meet the Queen after a concert at Ottawa's National Arts Centre in October 1977.

Frank Gunn/The Canadian Press

Aaron Harris/The Canadian Press

landmarks such as the Rockies and the Northwest Passage; and offbeat sights such as the world's largest Easter egg in Vegreville, Alberta.

The Queen has also visited Canadian landmarks located outside of Canada, such as the Vimy Ridge monument dedicated to Canadian First World War soldiers in France, and the Canadian military graveyards in Normandy.

Queen Elizabeth II has also established a very special relationship with the Royal Canadian Mounted Police, a truly iconic Canadian symbol. The Mounties escort her during all royal trips to Canada and, in return, she has attended many of their anniversary celebrations, and visited their training centre in Regina and their horse barns in Ottawa. In 2005, she offered

∧ Pianist Oscar Peterson, the king of Canadian jazz, greets the Queen at Roy Thomson Hall in Toronto following a concert in 2002.

condolences in person to family members of four Mounties slain by a gunman in Mayerthorpe, Alberta.

The Queen is also well versed in Canadian culture, a key feature on the agenda of many royal tours. In 1959, she took in Shakespeare's *As You Like It* at the Stratford Festival, and since then has visited the CBC headquarters, toured several Inuit sculpture gardens, and most likely seen the traditional dance of every ethnic community several times over.

∧ Robbie Baker (right) and Paul Langlois of the
Tragically Hip meet the Queen after a concert in
Toronto in 2002.

Frank Gunn/The Canadian Press

> If there's a giant Easter egg, then it must be Vegreville, Alberta. The Queen and Vegreville Mayor Larry Ruptash tour the huge egg in 1978, three years after it was built to mark the 100th anniversary of the RCMP.

∨ Premier Gary Doer and the Queen stroll past a giant representation of Manitoba's official symbol after a dinner in Winnipeg in 2002.

Adrian Wyld/The Canadian Press

Rod MacIvor/The Canadian Press

^ Canadian track athlete Diane Jones-Konihowski presents a baton to the Queen at the opening ceremonies of the 1978 Commonwealth Games in Edmonton. The baton contained an opening speech from the Queen, sent from Buckingham Palace. Jones-Konihowski, a member of the Canadian Olympic Sports Hall of Fame, went on to win a gold medal in the pentathlon at the Edmonton Games.

^ The Queen visits Grant Rennie on his farm near Regina in October 1988.

∧ The Queen and Prince Philip listen to speeches
at the Nunavut legislative assembly in Iqaluit in
2002. Although she has visited the Far North
several times, it was the Queen's first visit after the
creation of Nunavut as Canada's third territory.

www.cpimages.com

< Toronto Mayor David Crombie welcomes the Queen to city hall on June 26, 1973.

∨ The Queen watches participants in a cultural festival in Toronto in 2002.

Kevin Frayer/The Canadian Press

∧ Members of the Federation of Filipino-Canadians
meet the Queen in Toronto in 2002.

Frank Gunn/The Canadian Press

Wally Hayes/The Canadian Press

< The Queen and Prince Andrew get a lesson on pioneer traditions during a visit to Upper Canada Village in Morrisburg, Ontario, in 1976.

∨ The Queen arrives on Parliament Hill in an open landau during Canada Day celebrations in 1992. It was the country's 125th birthday.

∧ Retired Canadian Lt.-Gen. Romeo Dallaire (left)) and author Michael Ondaatje flank the Queen during a luncheon at Rideau Hall in 2002.

Adrian Wyld /The Canadian Press

> Nia Vardalos, writer and star of the movie *My Big Fat Greek Wedding*, has a chat with the Queen before an event in Vardalos' hometown of Winnipeg in 2002. The romantic comedy set records as the top-grossing independent film ever.

Paul Chiasson/The Canadian Press

^ Alberta Premier Ralph Klein follows the Queen out of the Alberta legislature in 2005.

> Former Canadian cyclist Louis Garneau puts his arm around the Queen while Garneau's wife takes their picture outside Rideau Hall in Ottawa in October 2002. The embrace was an apparent breach of royal protocol. The Queen, however, did not appear too upset. "I just put my arm around her shoulder," Garneau said later. "In sport, we do that all the time."

www.cpimages.com

Ron Poling/The Canadian Press

^ The Queen and Prince Philip participated in the
ceremony in the Senate on April 17, 1982 that
proclaimed Canada's independence from Britain.

< Alberta Premier Ralph Klein (left) introduces the Queen to the Alberta legislature in May 2005.

∨ The Queen officially opens Parliament in October 1977.

∧ The Queen addresses the Alberta legislature in 2005 during her visit to celebrate the province's centennial.

Paul Chiasson/The Canadian Press

< The Red Ensign comes down at the flag inaugura-
tion ceremony on Parliament Hill on February
15, 1965. It was replaced with the Maple Leaf.
Gov. Gen. Georges Vanier, Prime Minister Lester
Pearson, Opposition Leader John Diefenbaker, 600
prominent guests, and a crowd of several thousand
watched the historic moment.

v The Queen stands next to business tycoon Conrad
Black, dressed in the uniform of the honorary
colonel of the Governor General's Foot Guards,
as *O Canada* is played at Government House in
Ottawa in 1997.

^ The Queen picks up some quilting tips at a rural
fair in Sussex, New Brunswick, in 2002.

Andrew Vaughan/The Canadian Press

< The Queen and Lt.-Gov. David Lam of British Columbia take a walk through the garden at Government House in Victoria in August 1994.

> One of two beavers being presented to the Queen by Viscount Amory, governor of the Hudson's Bay Co., sneaks a peak at Her Majesty during a 1970 ceremony. The event was a repeat of an old tradition where the company paid two beavers to a ruling monarch when he or she visited the Canadian West.

∨ David Alan-Williams (left), captain of the *Matthew*, is greeted by Queen Elizabeth, Prince Philip and local Mayor Don Tremblett (right to left), in Bonavista, Newfoundland, in 1997. The voyage of the *Matthew* was a 500th-anniversary reenactment of John Cabot's arrival in North America.

Jacques Boissinot/The Canadian Press

Bill Croke/The Canadian Press

Ryan Remiorz/The Canadian Press

^ The Queen arrives at the opening ceremonies for
the 1994 Commonwealth Games in Victoria in a
1939 McLaughlin-Buick. The car was first used by
her father, King George VI, for his tour of Canada
in 1939.

< The Queen and Princess Anne check out the view
from a yacht en route to Victoria in 1971.

> Drummers greet the Queen during a tour of the
historic French fortress of Louisbourg on Cape
Breton Island, Nova Scotia, in 1994.

Andrew Vaughan/The Canadian Press

Adrian Wyld/The Canadian Press

www.cpimages.com

< The Golden Boy atop the Manitoba legislature is illuminated by fireworks during a ceremony for the Queen's visit to Winnipeg in 2002.

> The Queen inspects an Honour Guard in Regina during a memorial in May 2005 for four RCMP officers gunned down two months earlier in Mayerthorpe, Alberta.

Paul Chiasson/The Canadian Press

< With a push of a switch, the Queen officially starts the construction of the Expo 86 site in Vancouver in 1983. Prime Minister Pierre Trudeau and Senator Jack Austin observe.

Paul Chiasson/The Canadian Press

^ Spencer Gordon, son of slain RCMP officer Anthony Gordon, rests on his mother Kim's shoulder at a ceremony the Queen (background) attended in May 2005 to remember Gordon and three other Mounties shot to death in rural Alberta.

Kevin Frayer/The Canadian Press

∧ The Queen looks over participants in a festival in
Toronto in 2002.

< Portrait photographer Yousuf Karsh is shown at
his Ottawa studio in 1988 with an exposure he
created of Queen Elizabeth.

Dave Buston/The Canadian Press

Paul Chiasson/The Canadian Press

∧ Accompanied by federal Justice Minister Ray Hnatyshn, the Queen tours the Doukhobour Heritage Village in Veregin, Saskatchewan, in 1987.

< Followed by RCMP constables, the Queen makes her way to an interfaith church service on Parliament Hill in 2002.

> The Queen and Saskatchewan Premier Lorne Calvert take shelter under umbrellas during a visit to the Saskatchewan legislature in 2005.

CHAPTER 2

∧ The Queen presents new colours to the Governor General's Foot Guards during a ceremony in Ottawa in 1997.

< The Queen inspects an honour guard of the Royal Canadian Horse Artillery at Uplands Airport in Ottawa in 1982.

THE CANADIAN ARMED FORCES

T he Queen is a member of the generation that was shaped by the Second World War. Her family experienced the devastation of the Blitz first-hand, and as a young princess Elizabeth trained as a vehicle maintenance worker with the British army.

Whether it's because of this background or her constitutional role, recognition of those who serve their country has always been a huge part of the Queen's life. In virtually every visit to Canada, she has made sure to meet with our veterans. "She really appreciates the First World War veterans and what they have done," veteran Gilbert Davis, wounded in action at Vimy Ridge, said after meeting the Queen in Edmonton during a 1978 royal visit.

The Queen is also popular with high-ranking military officials. During her 1957 visit, it was reported that top army officers were angry because she was booked to inspect an air force and a navy guard of honour—but not an army guard of honour. The unification of Canada's Armed Forces in the 1960s has since alleviated these issues and must have been of great relief to the Queen and tour planners.

The Queen has helped mark major events in Canada's military history many times. In 1994, she helped Prime Minister Jean Chrétien dedicate the first major Canadian war memorial

∧ Veterans take part in an official departure ceremony at the Saddledome in Calgary in 2005.

Paul Chiasson/The Canadian Press

∧ The Queen inspects an honour guard during rainy centennial ceremonies at the Saskatchewan legislature in 2005.

∨ Another day, another honour guard: the Queen walks the line at centennial celebrations in Edmonton in 2005.

Jeff McIntosh/The Canadian Press

in Britain's Green Park, next to Buckingham Palace.

Ten years later, on the 60th anniversary of the Allies' D-Day assault into northern France, the Queen attended ceremonies at Courseulles-sur-Mer, where the Canadian troops landed. "Britain had been directly threatened by the enemy, but you came across the Atlantic from the relative security of your homeland to fight for the freedom of Europe," the Queen told the veterans gathered.

In April 2007, she helped re-dedicate Vimy Ridge, Canada's most celebrated European war monument, on the 90th anniversary of the famous First World War battle that killed 3,600 Canadians. "Those who seek the foundations of Canada's distinction would do well to begin here at Vimy," the Queen told a crowd of about 15,000, including Canadian war veterans and teens.

∧ The Queen attends ceremonies marking the 90th anniversary of the Battle of Vimy Ridge in April 2007. From left to right: Laureen Harper, wife of Prime Minister Stephen Harper, French Prime Minister Dominique de Villepin, the Queen, Stephen Harper, and the Duke of Edinburgh.

> The Queen arrives at a ceremony marking the 60th anniversary of D-Day in Courseulles-sur-Mer, France on June 6, 2004.

∨ Max Balinson, 6, has a chat with the Queen at a ceremony to present the Argyll and Sutherland Highlanders with new colours at Copps Coliseum in Hamilton, in 2002.

Tom Hanson/The Canadian Press

Kevin Frayer/The Canadian Press

In 1993, Queen Elizabeth II approved a Canadian version of the Victoria Cross, the highest award for valour that any Canadian Forces veteran can achieve. She also acts as honorary colonel-in-chief to Canadian regiments, including the Canadian Grenadier Guards, the Governor General's Foot Guards, the 48th Highlanders, the Royal Regiment of Canadian Artillery, the Argyll and Sutherland Highlanders, the Royal 22e Regiment, the Calgary Highlanders, and the Governor General's Horse Guards.

∧ Veterans get a close-up view of the Queen in
Edmonton in 2005.

^ > The Queen presents new colours to the Argyll and Sutherland Highlanders in Hamilton, Ontario, in 2002.

∧ Prime Minister Jean Chrétien and the Queen prepare to review the Princess Patricia Regiment from Edmonton at Buckingham Palace in London in 1998. It was the first time since 1953 that a Canadian regiment had guarded the palace.

∧ The Queen chats with Maj. Luc-Andre Racine, commander of a guard of honour from the Royal 22e Regiment during an inspection on Parliament Hill in 1992.

∧ The Queen and Lt.-Col. C.V. Carlson, parade
commander, inspect regiments receiving colours in
Parliament Hill ceremonies in 1967.

Lynn Ball/The Canadian Press

∧ Inspecting troops on Parliament Hill in 1967.

∨ The Queen and French President Jacques Chirac attend an international ceremony honouring veterans on the 60th Anniversary of D-Day at Arromanches, France in 2004.

Tom Hanson/The Canadian Press

< Prince Philip watches as the Queen signs the guest book at the Museum of the Regiments in Calgary in 2005.

∧ The Queen inspects an honour guard during a welcoming ceremony at the Saskatchewan legislature in 2005.

∧ The Queen with the Argyll and Sutherland Highlanders in Hamilton, Ontario, in 2002.

∧ With the Governor General's Foot Guards in
Ottawa in 1997.

∧ Inspecting a guard of honour at Canada Day celebrations on Parliament Hill in 1997.

Fred Chartrand/The Canadian Press

∧ The Queen, Prime Minister Jean Chrétien, and media mogul Conrad Black (right), greet veterans during a ceremony unveiling the Canada Memorial in London in 1994.

> With veterans during a wreath-laying ceremony at the war memorial in Ottawa in 2002.

Paul Chiasson/The Canadian Press

∧ Another Canada Day, another honour guard: the
Queen on Parliament Hill in 1990.

∧ Queen Elizabeth, the Queen Mother, was also a
popular honorary colonel of Canadian regiments.
Here she inspects an honour guard provided by
the Maritime Command at CFB Shearwater, Nova
Scotia, in 1979.

CHAPTER 3

> The Queen chats with Chief Justa Monk of the Tl'azt'en Nations in Prince George, B.C., in 1994. Behind the Queen is B.C. Premier Mike Harcourt.

Paul Chiasson/The Canadian Press

CANADA'S FIRST NATIONS

C anada's Aboriginal Peoples have long been prominent participants in royal tours. Usually, they will demonstrate some aspect of traditional aboriginal culture, as the British press is fond of pictures of the Queen with aboriginal chiefs in full feather. But the country's First Nations have occasionally managed to push the agenda beyond the "photo op" and onto their own concerns. The Queen, given her position as head of state, always steers away from publicly commenting on political issues (the words she speaks are usually written by the Canadian government) although she has spoken, repeatedly, about the value that the founding nations bring to Canada.

The Queen's visits with our First Nations have not always taken place without confrontation. One show of defiance occurred during a 1973 visit to Regina, when a chief criticized

< Chief Leonard Pelletier of the Fort William First Nations and the Queen watch aboriginal dancing in Thunder Bay, Ontario, in 1973.

Her Majesty's government for the "yoke of dependence" it had imposed on First Nations. The Queen merely murmured "thank you" in response to the man. The next day, during a speech in Calgary, she said "my government of Canada recognizes the importance of full compliance with the spirit and terms of your treaties."

In 1987, during a visit to British Columbia, a group of First Nations protesters accused the Queen of taking power over aboriginal lands. She appeared surprised by the protest but continued to wave to other spectators. In 1994, some native leaders in the Northwest Territories said they wouldn't meet with the Queen because they felt she was not supportive of the

∧ Chief Alphonse Bird of the Federation of Saskatchewan Indian Nations and the Queen visit First Nations University in Regina in 2005. The university offers undergraduate and graduate degrees within an environment of Indian culture and history.

> Accompanied by B.C. Premier Gordon Campbell, the Queen watches a Musqueam warriors dance at the University of British Columbia in 2002.

^ The Queen watches a dance of welcome performed in her honour at the aboriginal village at the Calgary Stampede in 1973.

fur trade. The Queen still visited Yellowknife, officially opening the Northwest Territories' first formal legislative building and meeting other aboriginal elders and community leaders. She earned the sympathy of at least one person, Marie Uviluq, who watched the Queen patiently shake hands and make small talk and then told her, "Your Majesty, you've got one tough gig."

Canada's aboriginal leaders have even attempted to meet the Queen on her own turf. In 1989, a group of Manitoba leaders visited Buckingham Palace to ask her to help bring post-secondary education to Canadian reserves. Her Majesty was not at home and a letter was left at the side door. Eight years later, Ovide Mercredi, national chief of the Assembly of First

> Dancers meet the Queen after a performance in Winnipeg in 2002.

∨ The Queen visits an Innu hunting tent in Sheshatshiu, Labrador, in 1997.

Nations, requested an audience with Queen Elizabeth II; she turned him down.

As in other communities, reaction to monarchy is mixed among Canada's aboriginal people. In 1997, when the Queen visited Bonavista, Newfoundland, to welcome the arrival of the *Matthew*, a ship that reenacted John Cabot's voyage to Canada, some aboriginals protested the celebrations, saying they overlooked the fact that Newfoundland's Beothuk Indians were exterminated by disease and clashes with the English settlers who followed Cabot. But the same Innu Nation welcomed the Queen days later to their community of Sheshatshiu during her first visit to Labrador. The community had spent several

Paul Chiasson/The Canadian Press

weeks cleaning up along the highways and had blue and white balloons tied to a bridge along the road to welcome her into town. She was invited to sample wild game and was presented with aboriginal artwork. "We wanted her to see the culture, our way of life, and the atmosphere of seeing Innu people," said Chief Paul Rich.

Resident Mary Pia Benuen added: "The way I see it, she is everybody's Queen. It's nice for her to know who the Innu are."

Paul Chiasson/The Canadian Press

Doug Ball/The Canadian Press

< First Nations chiefs talk to the Queen at Spruce Meadows near Calgary in 1990. She was presented with a petition asking for her help in their fight for self government.

> A young performer presents some royal entertainment. On the Queen's right is Paul Okalik, government leader of Nunavut. Prime Minister Jean Chrétien is behind them.

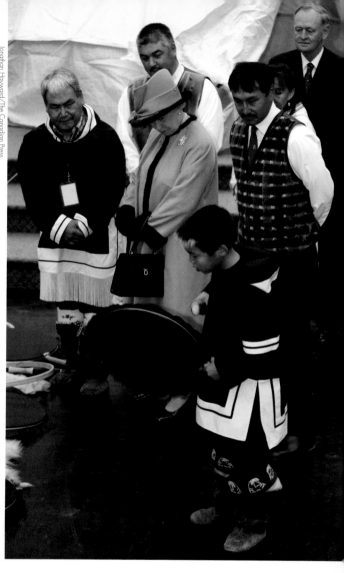

Jonathan Hayward/The Canadian Press

Paul Chiasson/The Canadian Press

< The Queen checks out a display of seal skins at the high school in Iqaluit in 2002.

∧ Accompanied by Chief Wellington Staats, the
   Queen meets children of the Six Nations Council
   of the Mohawks near Brantford, Ontario, in 1984.

Fred Chartrand/The Canadian Press

∧ The Queen meets elders inside an Innu hunting tent in Sheshatshiu, Labrador, in 1997.

Andrew Vaughan/The Canadian Press

> Chief Philomena Alphonse of the Coast Salish presents the Queen with a seating blanket at the opening ceremonies of the 1994 Commonwealth Games in Victoria.

< Just what he wanted: the Queen looks at moccasins given to Prince Philip, right, at First Nations University in Regina in 2005. Between the royal couple is university president Eber Hampton.

> Harold Cardinal, president of the Alberta Indian Association, watches the Queen emerge from a teepee at an Indian village in Calgary in 1973.

Paul Chiasson/The Canadian Press

Paul Chiasson/The Canadian Press

> Just what she wanted: the Queen is presented with a quilt by First Nations University president Hampton as Chief Alphonse Bird observes.

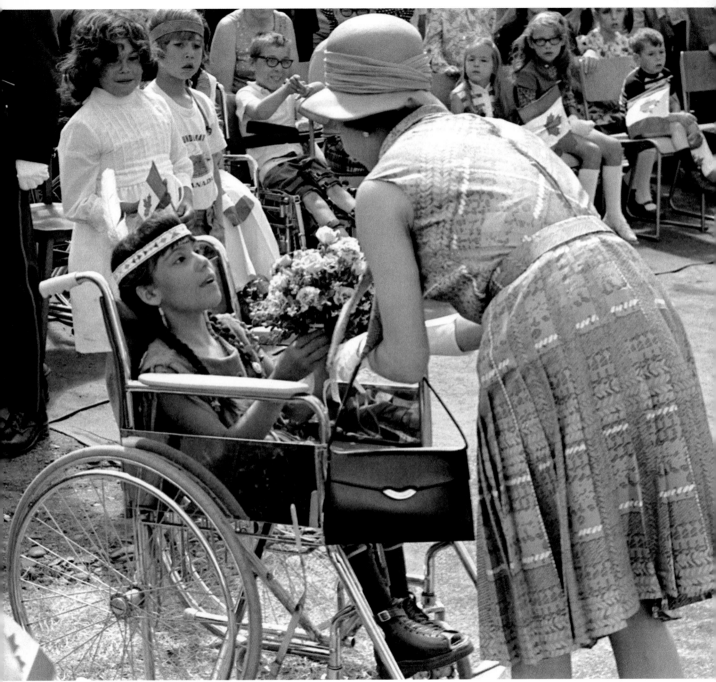

∧ Watching a traditional Inuit bone game in an Iqaluit school in 2002. Nunavut government leader Paul Okalik, centre, and school principal David Serkoak accompany the Queen.

∨ With Gov. Gen. Adrienne Clarkson and Prime Minister Jean Chrétien in Iqaluit in 2002.

< Trina Pelletier, 7, daughter of Chief Leonard Pelletier of the Fort William First Nations, presents the Queen with flowers in Thunder Bay, Ontario, in 1973.

www.cpimages.com

< The Queen and Princess Anne with Thomasina
  Emoralik during a visit to an Inuit settlement near
  Resolute Bay on Cornwallis Island in 1970.

> Chief R. Donald Maracle of the Bay of Quinte
  Mohawks presents the Queen with a feather at a
  festival in Toronto in 2002.

CHAPTER 4

Fred Chartrand/The Canadian Press

∧ To mark the death of the Queen's sister, Margaret, in February 2002, the Canadian flag flies at half-mast near a statue of Her Majesty on horseback on Parliament Hill.

< The Queen rides Burmese, a horse given to her by the Mounties, for the final time during the trooping of the colour in London in 1986.

HORSES AND HOUNDS

The Queen's love of horses is world renowned. Britons first knew her as a fair-haired little girl who played for hours with her "stable" of three dozen toy horses. Many of her visits to Canada have involved a trip to a racetrack or horse barn and there have been a number of horse trades between the Queen and her Canadian subjects.

In 1969, the Royal Canadian Mounted Police presented the Queen with Burmese, a sturdy black mare born in Saskatchewan. Burmese quickly endeared herself to the Queen, who for 12 years rode her sidesaddle in the annual Trooping the Colour parade, which marks the Queen's official birthday.

Burmese and the Queen became a familiar sight featured on postcards and have also been immortalized in a statue at the Regina legislature. Burmese distinguished herself—and her

∧ Corgis everywhere: the Queen talks with members of the Manitoba Corgi Association during a visit to Winnipeg in 2002.

RCMP trainers—in 1981 when she remained calm after a man fired five blank revolver shots at the Queen during the parade. Burmese retired in 1986 and the Queen started riding in a carriage instead of training another horse for the sidesaddle.

During a 1977 royal visit to Regina and to mark the force's 1973 centenary, the RCMP presented the Queen with another horse named Centenial, an offspring of the famous racehorse Man O' War. "He's so beautiful, he's so beautiful," said the

Queen, despite the fact that he kept turning his back to her. She also rode Centenial at the Trooping the Colour, and a larger-than-life bronze statue of the Queen atop Centenial sits on a knoll behind the Parliament Buildings in Ottawa.

In 1998, on their 125th anniversary, the RCMP gave the Queen a seven-year-old gelding named James. He was black with small white markings, known as socks, on three of his hooves. While the Queen never rode James in the Trooping the Colour parade, Prince Charles did.

∨ Prince Philip gives Princess Anne a few tips before she competes in the equestrian event at the Montreal Olympics in 1976. The Queen, Prince Charles, and Prince Andrew listen in.

Four years later, the Queen presented the RCMP with an Irish black mare named Golden Jubilee in honour of her 50th anniversary on the throne. The horse, selected personally by the Queen, is the same type used in her household cavalry and also drew the Queen Mother's funeral carriage.

Equestrian events often appear on the royal schedule during trips to Canada, including three trips to Toronto for the Queen's Plate, Canada's best known horse race. The race was named after the Queen's great-great-grandmother, Queen Victoria, although Victoria, unlike Queen Elizabeth II, was not especially known for her horse-racing enthusiasm. In 1997, the last time the Queen attended, she presented the winner's trophy to an exuberant Frank Stronach, an auto parts magnate, whose horse, Awesome Again, strode victoriously across the finish line.

The Queen's passion for animals does not end with horses. Her world-famous love of corgis, small, short-legged, Welsh dogs, is shared by many Canadians, who often trot out their pets to see the Queen during her royal visits.

In Edmonton in 2005, the Queen visited with Jennifer Hancock of the Welsh Corgi Association of Canada and her seven dogs. "She was very sweet," said Hancock. "She took the time to say hello and be with them and wanted to know all their names."

∧ A laugh at the track: the Queen and Prince Philip leave Woodbine Racetrack in Toronto in 1973 after the 114th running of the Queen's Plate.

www.cpimages.com

Kevin Frayer/The Canadian Press

∧ The Queen watches as jockey Mike Smith celebrates his victory aboard Awesome Again in the 138th running of the Queen's Plate in 1997.

< King George VI and Queen Elizabeth attend the Queen's Plate in 1939 at Woodbine Race Course. Their visit began the royal tradition.

Frank Gunn/The Canadian Press

> Smith receives congratulations from the Queen as Awesome Again's owner, Frank Stronach, watches.

> Representatives from the Queen's favourite dog breed turn out to greet her at the Alberta legislature in 2005.

^ E.P. Taylor, president of the Ontario Jockey Club, escorts the Queen at Woodbine in 1973.

Paul Chiasson/The Canadian Press

∧ The Queen visits the RCMP musical ride headquarters in Ottawa in 2002.

> Royal present: Her Majesty presents RCMP com-
missioner Giuliano Zaccardelli with Golden Jubilee,
a horse intended for the RCMP musical ride, in
2002.

> ∧ Gift horse: the RCMP present a horse named Centenial to the Queen at the RCMP training depot at Regina in 1973.

> < Cpl. Bill Stewart of the RCMP musical ride boards James the horse on a trailer bound for England. The RCMP gave the horse to the Queen in honour of its 125th anniversary.

> > U.S. President Ronald Reagan, left, on Centenial and the Queen, on Burmese, ride on the grounds of Windsor Castle in 1982.

Bob Dougherty/The Associated Press

Ron Poling/The Canadian Press

www.cpimages.com

∧ Time of Plenty, one of the horses entered in the
114th Queen's Plate, catches the Queen's eye at
Woodbine Racetrack in 1973.

< With Prime Minister Brian Mulroney, the Queen
unveils a statue on Parliament Hill in 1992 that
depicts her riding her horse Centenial.

< ∧ At the 2005 unveiling of the Golden Jubilee statue at the Saskatchewan legislature that shows the Queen riding Burmese.

> The Queen and Prince Philip watch a riding demonstration at an agricultural fair in Sussex, New Brunswick, in 2002.

CHAPTER 5

The Queen and Gov. Gen. Adrienne Clarkson leave a tree-planting ceremony at Rideau Hall in 2002.

THE QUEEN AND HER MINISTERS

The Queen is Canada's head of state, but it is the governor general who carries out Her Majesty's daily duties in Canada. She has had a close relationship with each governor general who has served during her 50-plus years on the throne. Unlike those of previous monarchs, the Queen's representatives have all been Canadians. She took the throne the same month as Governor General Vincent Massey, the first Canadian appointed to the post, began his term, and since then the governor general has always been a Canadian citizen, recommended to the Queen by the prime minister.

The Queen has also worked with more than 10 Canadian prime ministers. Her relationship with some was close, but with others, it was more formal. Lester Pearson was one of those with whom she held a close relationship. In his memoirs, Pearson wrote that he was flattered when told by Michael Adeane, the Queen's secretary, that she considered him a "close and valued" friend. Pearson described Her Majesty as a "particularly attractive and agreeable lady" away from the cameras, and knowledgeable about Canadian issues. He recalled that in

< The Queen and Gov. Gen. Georges Vanier visit the Citadel in Quebec City in 1964.

> ^ Prime Minister Pierre Trudeau and the Queen attend a dinner in Vancouver in 1983.

1964, during the stress-filled visit when the Queen's life was threatened by Quebec separatists, she was calm, although she couldn't understand why the situation had created such headlines, especially in Britain. She was also "quite stage-struck" when she met Canadian actor Lorne Greene, of TV's *Bonanza*, at a variety show in Charlottetown during that trip. (Apparently the royal family watched *Bonanza* every Sunday night just like most Canadians at the time.) At a meeting in London in late

> Montreal Mayor Jean Drapeau talks to the Queen at a reception at Montreal city hall in July 1976, just before she opened the Olympic Games.

Hayes/The Canadian Press

^ Gov. Gen. Michaelle Jean and her daughter, Marie-Eden, meet the Queen at Balmoral Castle in Scotland in 2005.

< P.E.I. Premier Alex Campbell and the Queen walk through downtown Charlottetown on Canada Day 1973, also the day ceremonies began for the Island's centennial.

1967, she revealed to Pearson she was anxious that the monarchy not be the cause of a division in Canadian unity. "I was moved by her attitude and her sensitive understanding of the changing situation," Pearson wrote.

The media were always looking for trouble between the Queen and Pierre Trudeau, who followed Pearson. He was famous for doing a pirouette behind her back during a photo session at Buckingham Palace in London in 1977, which

> The Queen and Prime Minister Lester Pearson take a site tour atop the mini-rail at Expo 67 in Montreal.

^ Prime Minister Jean Chrétien and the Queen at Canada Day ceremonies in 1997.

< The Queen and Chrétien leave a church service in Ottawa in 2002 during her Golden Jubilee tour.

gave him a largely undeserved reputation as being anti-royal. A year later, he was criticized by British media for "sunning himself" on a Mediterranean beach while a royal tour began in Canada. In truth, Governor General Jules Léger was on hand to greet the Queen. Rumours intensified about the poor relationship between the Queen and Trudeau when the two seemed to exchange few words at a couple of public events later in the tour. (On the same royal visit, Trudeau took Prince Andrew to a disco in Ottawa where they danced well past midnight.) Michael Shea, the Queen's press secretary, called the rumours

www.cpimages.com

< Prime Minister John Diefenbaker, known for his strong support for the monarchy, bows to the Queen at a reception in Ottawa in 1957.

"total rubbish." Trudeau later wrote in his memoirs that he "was always impressed not only by the grace she displayed in public at all times, but by the wisdom she showed in private conversation."

In 1984, another Liberal prime minister, John Turner, risked the displeasure of the Queen, not to mention losing the vote of monarchists, when he flew to London to ask her to postpone a

v The Queen presents Alberta Lt.-Gov. Norman Kwong with the Knight of the Order of Saint John as his wife Mary looks on in Edmonton in 2005.

Paul Chiasson/The Canadian Press

∧ Premier Bernard Lord of New Brunswick and the Queen share a laugh as she arrives in Fredericton during her 2002 visit.

< Governor-General Jules Léger strolls with the Queen through the grounds of Government House in Ottawa in 1977. In the background are Léger's wife Gabrielle and Prince Philip.

Andrew Vaughan/The Canadian Press

summer visit so an election could be called. Perhaps he hoped he could get away with it because of his friendly relationship with her sister, Princess Margaret. In 1958, when he was a young lawyer, he had danced and chatted with Margaret at a ball given in her honour in British Columbia, causing tongues to wag. The Queen moved her visit to the fall, but by then Turner had lost the election and it was Prime Minister Brian Mulroney who did the meeting and greeting.

It was a provincial premier, not a prime minister, however, who created the biggest headlines connected with a royal tour. Richard Hatfield, premier of New Brunswick from 1970 to 1987, doted on the Queen and the royal family. He would try to be on his best behaviour during royal visits but his ebullience and excitement would occasionally carry him over the top, recalls Chris Morris, long-time Canadian Press correspondent in Fredericton who covered the Queen's visit to New Brunswick in 1984. The visit itself was largely uneventful, until RCMP officers discovered a small bag of marijuana in Hatfield's suitcase during a routine search of luggage being loaded on the plane carrying the Queen from Fredericton to Moncton. Hatfield had been given a seat on the plane at the last minute and he happily joined the royal entourage. "However, he seemed tense and distracted

^ > Tree-planting is a royal tradition in Ottawa. Above, the Queen plants an oak tree at the end of her 1977 visit. Right, she adds another tree to the grounds at Rideau Hall in 2002.

< The Queen and Gov. Gen. Adrienne Clarkson arrive for a tree-planting ceremony at Rideau Hall in Ottawa in 2002.

once in Moncton," said Morris. The police kept quiet about the drugs for several weeks, then all hell broke loose when Hatfield was formally charged with possession of marijuana and forced to stand trial. He was eventually acquitted but the incident cemented his image as Disco Dick and soured his relationship with the public. In the 1987 election, Hatfield's Progressive Conservative Party lost every seat to the Liberals.

< The Queen, Saskatchewan Premier Lorne Calvert, sculptor Susan Veldor, and RCMP commissioner Giuliano Zaccardelli watch the unveiling of a statue in front of the Saskatchewan legislature in 2005. The statue depicts the Queen riding Burmese, a horse given to her by the RCMP.

^ Prime MInister Brian Mulroney and his wife, Mila, greet the Queen at a state dinner in Winnipeg in 1984.

< Duff, Gov. Gen. Vincent Massey's golden retriever, carries the Queen's purse during a stroll around the garden at Rideau Hall in 1957.

> The Queen and Prime Minister Paul Martin arrive in Edmonton for an official dinner, part of Alberta's 100th-birthday celebrations, in 2005.

Jeff McIntosh/The Canadian Press

Doug Ball/The Canadian Press

^ After a goodbye state dinner, the Queen walks with Gov. Gen. Roland Michener down the red carpet to her aircraft at Uplands Airport in Ottawa in July 1967.

Dave Buston/The Canadian Press

^ Gov. Gen. Jeanne Sauvé meets the Queen at Victoria Airport in 1987.

< Prime Minister Paul Martin (right) bids farewell to the Queen in Calgary in 2005.

> Prime Minister Pierre Trudeau and the Queen at B.C. Place Stadium in 1983.

Jeff McIntosh/The Canadian Press

Peter Bregg/The Canadian Press

Ron Poling/The Canadian Press

∧ At the 1978 Commonwealth Games in Edmonton. From left to right: Alberta Premier Peter Lougheed, Games Foundation chairman Sir Alex Ross, the Queen, Prime Minister Pierre Trudeau, Prince Philip.

> Pierre and Margaret Trudeau welcome Her Majesty at Toronto airport in 1973.

< The Queen with Prince Philip and Prime Minister Pierre Trudeau at 24 Sussex Drive on April 16, 1982, on the eve of the historic Constitution signing ceremony.

∧ The Queen speaks at a state dinner at Rideau Hall in 1977. Prime Minister Pierre Trudeau is to the right.

∧ Prime Minister Pierre Trudeau covers his ears to block the takeoff noise as the jet carrying the Queen leaves Ottawa in 1977.

> Prime Minister Pierre Trudeau performs his famous pirouette at Uplands Airport in Ottawa in 1982, following the Queen's departure after proclaiming the Constitution Act.

< The Queen and Prime Minister Brian Mulroney take their places in the royal box at a government-arranged gala in Toronto in 1984.

∨ The Queen, accompanied by Gerda Hnatyshyn (left), wife of Gov. Gen. Ray Hnatyshyn, Prime Minister Brian Mulroney and his wife Mila, look at a statue of the Queen on horseback as it is unveiled on Parliament Hill in 1992.

Fred Chartrand/The Canadian Press

Mike Blake/The Canadian Press

^ A portrait of the Queen is seen behind Conservative Leader Stephen Harper as he speaks to media in Guelph, Ontario, in 2004.

Larry MacDougal/The Canadian Press

< Goodbye: the Queen gives her famous wave during a departure ceremony at the Saddledome in Calgary in 2005. Gov. Gen. Adrienne Clarkson and her husband John Ralston Saul look on.

> Prime Minister Paul Martin applauds following a speech by the Queen at a dinner in Edmonton in 2005.

v Hello: Prime Minister Jean Chrétien greets the Queen as they arrive for a state dinner in Gatineau, Quebec, in 2002.

Tom Hanson/The Canadian Press

Paul Chiasson/The Canadian Press

< The Queen, Alberta Premier Ralph Klein, and his wife Colleen at the Alberta legislature in 2005.

> Opposition Leader Joe Clark and wife Maureen McTeer say goodbye to the Queen at Ottawa Airport in 1977. During Clark's brief tenure as prime minister in 1979 the Queen did not visit.

Fred Chartrand/The Canadian Press.

∧ The Queen and Prince Philip wave goodbye at the conclusion of their visit to Ottawa in 1977.

< Prime Minister Pierre Trudeau greets the Queen as she arrives in Ottawa for her 1982 visit to sign over the Constitution. Gov. Gen. Ed Schreyer and his wife Lily look on.

^ Prime Minister Paul Martin and his wife, Sheila, wave as the plane carrying the Queen departs Calgary for the United Kingdom in 2005.

CHAPTER 6

> Prince Charles and Princess Diana, with their sons Prince William (left) and Prince Harry, bid goodbye to a cheering Toronto crowd from aboard the royal yacht *Britannia* in 1991.

Hans Deryk/The Canadian Press

THE QUEEN'S FAMILY IN CANADA

< A security guard just behind Prince Charles's shoulder doesn't stop a woman from reaching out for a royal kiss as he and Princess Diana meet Canadians in Saint John, New Brunswick, in 1983.

The Queen's children were introduced to Canada at an early age, unlike previous generations of royals. The kids—Charles, Anne, Andrew, and Edward—have all visited Canada regularly, and Andrew attended Lakefield College School in Peterborough, Ontario. The Queen had wanted Charles to attend school in Canada but feared the Canadian media would not leave him alone. Charles's sons, William and Harry, have visited Canada several times. Their mother, Diana, the Princess of Wales, took them on the famous *Maid of the*

^ Prince Charles walks with junior Canadian rangers on a portion of the Trans Canada Trail in Mayo, Yukon, in 2001.

Mist ferry in Niagara Falls, Ontario and their father skied with them in Whistler, British Columbia. Harry was also posted in Alberta as part of his army training.

Charles has visited almost as many parts of Canada as his mother, with a particular fondness for the North; Anne has tramped through horse barns and Olympic training facilities; Andrew has danced in Ottawa discotheques (with Prime Minister Pierre Trudeau); and Edward has toured a french fry factory on Prince Edward Island.

> Prince Charles gets a little muddy 930 metres underground in a gold mine in Yellowknife, N.W.T., in 1975.

Doug Ball/The Canadian Press

The Queen's children first visited Canada in 1970. Charles started the tour in Ottawa and then flew to Frobisher Bay in the Northwest Territories to meet his mother, father, and sister. Wearing parkas given to them, they crossed the region by plane, visiting Inuit villages, oil exploration sites and a pingo— a huge [dome-shaped] ice mound covered by earth—in which Inuit were building a curling rink. The next major visit as a family, this time involving the entire clan, was in 1976, when they came to watch Anne compete in equestrian events at the Montreal Olympics.

There have been other notable visits by the Queen's children, including:

- Tours by Charles and Diana in 1983, 1986, and 1991. Diana created headlines wherever she went. In 1983, the couple made their first trip to Canada after their fairy-tale wedding two years earlier. In 1986, Diana had a dizzy spell while touring Expo 86, setting off rumours she was pregnant. She was not, but Charles later joked that she was "about to have sextuplets, which is really why she fainted." In 1991, amidst rumours of marital strife, the couple brought their sons, then nine and seven, who made their first public appearances outside of Britain.

- A 1998 visit by Charles, William, and Harry to Vancouver and Whistler, British Columbia. William, then 15, was dogged by squealing teenage girls. It was his first trip abroad after his mother's death.

- A visit by Edward and Sophie, the Earl and Countess of Wessex, in 2000 to Prince Edward Island. It was their first state visit to Canada and a test to see whether they could make up for the less-than-fairy-tale marriages of the older Windsor siblings.

From her base in Fredericton, Canadian Press correspondent Chris Morris earned the distinction of covering visits of all four of the Queen's children. In particular, she remembers Princess Anne's arrival in 1986 at the Fredericton airport. "Due to an oversight, a coffin containing the body of a New Brunswick resident who died while out of the province had been left on the tarmac awaiting retrieval by a funeral home. The funeral director was late and when Princess Anne stepped off the plane, no one could help noticing the casket off to one side. It was a grim addition to the usual welcome committee!" Later in the visit, Anne visited Canadian Forces Base Gagetown, where hot,

∧ Escorted by Premier John Buchanan, Queen Elizabeth, the Queen Mother, waves to people in Halifax in 1979.

> Despite a slight drizzle, Charles and Diana tour in an open jeep in Halifax in 1983.

Bob Carroll/The Canadian Press

> The Princess of Wales is saluted by a Mountie in Summerside, P.E.I., in 1983.

∨ Diana thanks her motorcycle police escort in Ottawa at the end of her visit in 1983.

Peter Bregg/The Canadian Press

dry weather made use of the firing range tricky because of the threat of fires. "But military brass wanted to give the princess a close-up look at tanks and guns so she was outfitted in combats and allowed to fire off one of the big guns at the range," recalls Morris. "When smoke refused to clear after one of her volleys, I remember a distraught-looking soldier running over to the fire tower near where I was standing, falling on his knees and saying 'Please, please tell me she hasn't started a forest fire.' If she did, it was quickly put out."

Murray Bray/The Canadian Press

∧ Prince Charles officiates at the crowning of
Laverna McMaster, 18, of Cluny, Alberta, as
Canada's "Indian princess for 1970." McMaster
sticks her tongue out in excitement.

∧ Charles dons a Canadian Olympic team hat at
an environmental heritage event in Vancouver in
1998.

> Charles visits the statue of runner Terry Fox below
Parliament Hill in 2001.

∧ Charles dances with Gabrielle Léger, wife of
Gov. Gen. Jules Léger, at an Ottawa ball in 1975.

< Norah Michener, wife of Gov. Gen. Roland
Michener (centre), curtsies to Prince Charles in
Winnipeg in 1970.

∧ Prince Charles visits the Dovercourt Boys and
Girls Club in Toronto in 1996.

Moe Doiron/The Canadian Press

Doug Ball/The Canadian Press

Doug Ball/The Canadian Press

∧ Garbed in a wolverine-trimmed parka and a rabbit fur hat, Prince Charles watches an ice house building competition in Frobisher Bay in 1975.

> Prince Charles is pulled by a team of sled dogs during his visit to Colville Lake, N.W.T., in 1975.

< Charles tests out a snowmobile during a visit to Pangnirtung, now part of Nunavut, in 1975.

Doug Ball/The Canadian Press

Adrian Wyld/The Canadian Press

∧ Charles arrives with Chief Perry Bellegarde at
ceremonies at Wanuskewin Heritage Park near
Saskatoon in 2001. It was his first visit to
Saskatchewan.

< Elder Gordon Oakes presents Prince Charles
with a blanket during a naming ceremony at
Wanuskewin Heritage Park near Saskatoon in
2001. The prince was given the Cree name The
Sun Watches over Him in a Good Way.

Ryan Remiorz/The Canadian Press

<^ Margaret Trudeau, wife of Prime Minister Pierre Trudeau, talks to Prince Charles at a reception also attended by the Queen in Ottawa in 1976. Left: Prince Andrew is shown in the background.

< Prince Charles and Margaret Trudeau, wife of Prime Minister Pierre Trudeau, attend a concert at the National Arts Centre in Ottawa in 1975.

www.cpimages.com

< Diana meets children in Victoria in 1986.

> Charles and Diana, followed by Archbishop Douglas Hambidge, at Christ Church Cathedral in Vancouver in 1986.

v Diana and Charles in Ottawa in 1983.

Chris Schwarz/The Canadian Press

C. Shwarz/The Canadian Press

> The Princess of Wales talks with singer Bryan Adams after a gala rock concert at the Expo Theatre in Vancouver in 1986.

Ryan Remiorz/The Canadian Press

Ron Poling/The Canadian Press

∧ Diana stands in a reception line in Ottawa before a dinner in 1983.

< Diana and Charles at the Chateau Laurier Hotel in Ottawa in 1983.

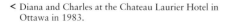

∧ A young girl gives the Princess of Wales a bouquet of flowers as the princess and Charles arrive in Summerside, P.E.I., in 1983.

< Diana meets Mi'kmaq women in Charlo, New Brunswick, in 1983.

> Diana visits Kelowna, B.C., in 1986.

Ron Poling/The Canadian Press

∧ Diana and sons Harry (left) and William ride on the *Maid of the Mist* tour boat in Niagara Falls, Ontario, in 1991.

< Diana visits Kelowna, British Columbia, in 1986.

∧ Prince William (left) jokes with his father, Prince
Charles, after being presented with a jacket and
hat from the Canadian Olympic team uniform in
Vancouver in 1998.

Chuck Stoody/The Canadian Press

> Well-wishers wait for Prince Charles to arrive in Assiniboia, Saskatchewan, in 2001.

∨ Prince Harry arrives at a school in Burnaby, B.C., in 1998.

> Amber White, 16, of Petawawa, Ontario, holds up a message for Prince William during a visit to Ottawa by his father in 2001.

^ Girls try to get Prince William to shake their hands
  in Burnaby, B.C., in 1998.

Frank Gunn/The Canadian Press

Joe Bryksa/The Canadian Press

∧ Princess Anne attends a dedication ceremony at the Health Sciences Centre in Winnipeg in 1999.

> Princess Anne at the 1976 Olympics with her horse, Goodwill.

< Green hat day: Princess Anne and Agriculture Minister Eugene Whelan, wearing his trademark green hat, at the Experimental Farm in Ottawa in 1982.

www.cpimages.com

∧ Princess Anne tours the equestrian venue at the Pan Am Games in Winnipeg in 1999.

< Princess Anne, colonel-in-chief of the regiment, inspects the Royal Regina Rifles in Regina in 2007.

∧ Anne rides dressage during the opening day of the
equestrian event at the 1976 Montreal Olympics.

Blaise Edwards/The Canadian Press

Dave Buston/The Canadian Press

∧ The Duchess of York at the paddle during her canoe trip with her husband in the Northwest Territories in 1987.

< Prince Andrew practises with his Lakefield College ski team at Cedar Mountain, Ontario, in 1977.

> Andrew, the Duke of York, gets a warm welcome to Toronto from Mila Ten, one of a group of dancers, in 1987.

> Prince Andrew and Sarah attend the 128th running of the Queen's Plate horse race in Toronto on July 19, 1987.

∨ Escorted by Ontario Premier David Peterson, Sarah, the Duchess of York, tours Old Fort William in Thunder Bay, Ontario, in 1987.

Dave Buston/The Canadian Press

Dave Buston/The Canadian Press

< Prince Andrew fires a starter pistol to begin a cross country race at Lakefield College in 1992. The prince was attending the homecoming of the Ontario college, which he attended in 1977.

Tim Clark/The Canadian Press

The Duke and Duchess of York, nearing their first wedding anniversary, play tourist in Niagara Falls, Ontario, in 1987. Left: the royal couple poses with the Horseshoe Falls in the background. Below: they take a ride aboard the tour boat *Maid of the Mist*.

Dave Buston/The Canadian Press

< ∨ Below: Prince Edward throws out the ceremonial first pitch prior to a baseball game between the Toronto Blue Jays and the Baltimore Orioles in Toronto in 2003. Left: The prince is escorted off the field by shortstop Chris Woodward of the Blue Jays.

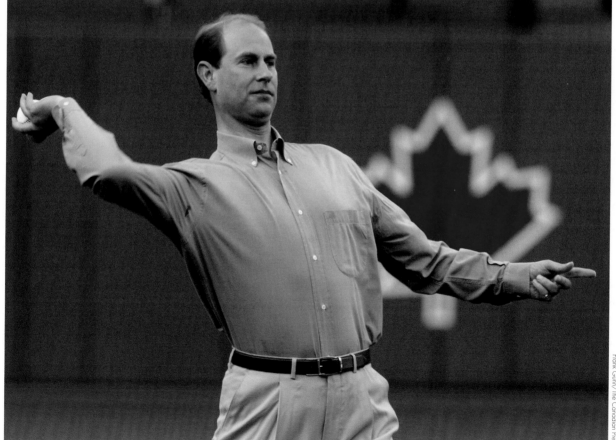

Kevin Frayer/The Canadian Press

Andrew Vaughan/The Canadian Press

∧ The Earl and Countess of Wessex at the Rodd Brudenell River Resort in Brudenell, P.E.I., in 2000.

< Prince Edward (left) and his wife Sophie, Countess of Wessex, arrive at the Edmonton Airport in 2001.

∧ The Earl and Countess of Wessex board a Canadian Forces Griffon helicopter at the Rodd Brudenell
River Resort in Brudenell, P.E.I., in 2000.

∧ Edward and Sophie arrive for a dinner hosted by the Canadian government in Charlottetown in 2000.

< Edward and Sophie check out the french fries produced at the Cavendish Farms processing plant in New Annan, P.E.I., in 2000.

∧ Queen Elizabeth, the Queen Mother, attends
Canada Day celebrations in Toronto in 1979.

CHAPTER 7

THE ELEMENTS

< The Queen, wearing uncharacteristic—but appropriate for the weather—knee-high boots, struggles into a raincoat at Keewatin Community College in The Pas in 1970. A light drizzle followed the royal family most of the day as they visited the northern Manitoba town.

> The Queen and the Duke of Edinburgh, each with an umbrella, greet people in Lumsden, Saskatchewan, in 2005. The visit, to help Saskatchewan and Alberta celebrate their 100th birthdays, was plagued by bad weather.

Jeff McIntosh/The Canadian Press

From torrential rain to brilliant sunshine, from the marrow-chilling temperatures of the North to the hot humidity of an Ontario summer, the Queen has experienced a wide range of Canadian weather during her years visiting the country.

Although most of her visits are scheduled for the better-weather months in the spring, summer, and fall, Mother Nature doesn't bow to the Queen. Then again, the Queen doesn't bow to Mother Nature either. In 2005, the 79-year-old monarch

∧ The Queen stands beneath her umbrella for the national anthem during rainy Alberta centennial celebrations at Commonwealth Stadium in Edmonton in 2005. She usually carries a clear umbrella so crowds can still see her, despite the weather.

earned admiration for stoically battling cold, driving rain virtually everywhere she toured in Alberta and Saskatchewan. "I ended up dubbing her a 'jolly good sport' in one story because she gracefully took the situation in stride," said reporter Michelle MacAfee, who covered the visit for The Canadian Press. "During one particularly steady, hard downpour, she walked along at a leisurely pace, shaking hands and accepting flowers, all to the delight of the hundreds of admirers who had been waiting several hours for a good position."

Her tolerance for rain is likely understandable given her British upbringing. But on her first visit to Canada, in October 1951, she showed she could be unsettled by snow. In Moose

> The wind tugs at the Queen's dress and threatens to take away her hat as she walks across the tarmac at Canadian Forces Base Namao, near Edmonton, in 1978. The Queen wears two hatpins to keep her headgear in place.

Paul Chiasson/The Canadian Press

Jaw, Saskatchewan, as former mayor Louis Lewry bowed to greet her, she snapped up his head by saying, "Ooh, the snow is running down my back." Perhaps that explains why 51 years later, in 2002, she wore a long fur coat on a visit to Winnipeg in early October.

Wind can sometimes be more disruptive than snow during a royal tour. In 1978, the Queen was greeted with 30 kilometre-an-hour winds in St. John's, Newfoundland, and in 1987 freezing wind was also a visitor on the tour. But no hats went flying—the Queen always ensures hers are held securely in place.

Throughout the years, the Queen has most impressed Canadians with her ability to look cool in intolerable heat, even while dressed in a long-sleeved coat and dress complete with gloves and hat. During a six-week, coast-to-coast visit in 1959, sticky weather was rampant. Crowds were suffering but the royal couple managed to look unruffled. In Regina, Saskatchewan, the Queen, wearing a coat and dress of peacock blue, spent five hours in the hot prairie sun at seven official functions.

Rod Maclvor/The Canadian Press

Even at its hottest, however, Canadian heat must seem like nothing to the Queen when compared with the conditions she has endured touring other Commonwealth countries. During a tour of Ceylon on a gruelling sticky day in the 1950s, she wore her coronation dress, which features emblems, crystals, diamonds, and pearls, and weighs more than 13 kilograms. "She passed within a few feet and my eyes searched her face," wrote journalist Frank Harvey in *Weekend Magazine*. "I saw only a serenely cool woman with not one bead of moisture on her skin."

∧ The Queen departs Parliament Hill following an interfaith service in Ottawa in 2002.

^ Another day, another legislature, more rain: the Queen arrives at the Saskatchewan legislature in 2005.

> The Queen cuts a cake representing the Alberta legislature during rainy provincial centennial celebrations in Edmonton in 2005.

^ An aide holds an umbrella over the Queen as she speaks during welcoming ceremonies at the Saskatchewan legislature in 2005.

< Dressed for cold, the Queen talks with Manitoba Premier Gary Doer at an outdoor stage in Winnipeg in 2002.

> The wind turns the Queen's umbrella inside out at the legislature buildings in Victoria in 1983.

Tom Hanson/The Canadian Press

> The Queen accepts a damp rose as she leaves Parliament Hill in 2002.

< With Gov. Gen. Adrienne Clarkson at the Saskatchewan legislature in 2005.

∨ The Queen at rainy Alberta centennial celebrations in Edmonton in 2005.

Paul Chiasson/The Canadian Press

< People stand in the rain waiting for the arrival of Her Majesty on Parliament Hill in 2002.

> The Queen keeps an umbrella close as she reviews the Princess Patricia Canadian Light Infantry in Victoria, B.C., in 1983.

∨ At a wet wreath-laying ceremony at the war memorial in Ottawa in 2002.

Paul Chiasson/The Canadian Press

Mike Blake/The Canadian Press

www.cpimages.com

< A rug is quickly thrown down over a muddy field at the Calgary Stampede in 1951 as Princess Elizabeth exits a stage coach. Assisting her is Jim Cross, president of the Calgary Stampede.

> Rain makes for a wet welcoming ceremony for the Queen at the Saskatchewan legislature in 2005.

∨ A gust of wind whips the sashes on the Queen's dress as she talks with an unidentified woman in the paddock area of Woodbine Racetrack in Toronto in 1973.

www.cpimages.com

Jeff McIntosh/The Canadian Press

Paul Chiasson/The Canadian Press

ʌ Fur for the cold; an umbrella for the wet: the
Queen is dressed for all weather at Commonwealth Stadium in Edmonton in 2005. Behind her
is Alberta Premier Ralph Klein.

< Prime Minister Pierre Trudeau appears to be
asking the Queen for umbrella space during Parliament Hill church services in 1977.

∧ The Queen at the Royal York Hotel in Toronto in 2002.

CHAPTER 8

∧ The hippies of the late 1960s and early 1970s who invented the term flower power would have approved the hat worn by the Queen in British Columbia in 1971.

HER HATS

F eathers. Fur. Flowers. Frills. Whether it's because she's English, a lady of a certain age, or just because she likes to have something on her head, you can count on the Queen to wear a hat.

The Queen has never been known as a fashion setter, but for hats she is tops, according to Karyn Gingras, owner of Lilliput Hats in Toronto. Gingras approves of the Queen's taste in hats, saying they are mostly well designed and flattering. "Her hats are pretty cutting edge—conservatively cutting edge," Gingras said in 2002, on the eve of the Queen's visit to Canada.

The Queen rarely appears without some sort of headgear: hats for daytime occasions, tiaras for evening events, kerchiefs for around the castle grounds. She even wore a hat to her son Edward's wedding, in 1999, after guests had been asked not to. The official line was that her lilac feather-and-pearls concoction was actually a "headdress."

Her hats have similar characteristics. She is fond of a turban style that is made of the same material as her dress, or dyed to match. She also likes a turned-up brim, which ensures that there is no distance between her and others, and also keeps photographers happy because wide-brimmed hats put the wearer's face in shadow.

<A furry-headed Queen talks to Canadian rowers at Dow Lake in Ottawa in 1977.

>A woven straw hat she wore in Vancouver in 1983 was a departure from her usual look.

∨The Queen is often seen in brimmed hats that don't hide her face, yet protect from the bright sunlight—such as this yellow-brimmed hat she wore to the Calgary military museum in 1990.

The Queen has made some hat mistakes, admits Gingras. There was a yellow, wide-brimmed stetson-like hat worn during her Jubilee in 2002. And sometimes the Queen will wear a dramatic-angled style that doesn't suit her. But usually she gets it right.

She has had the best milliners in the world to pick from. Of course, the hat industry is well supported in Britain, where women routinely wear hats to such functions as weddings and funerals. During the Royal Ascot, a horseracing event held annually in the United Kingdom, women actually compete for the title of most outrageous hat on Ladies Day. The hats the Queen wears to Ascot are of such interest that bookmakers take bets on what colour they will be.

Chuck Stoody/The Canadian Press

< The Queen in an elegant fedora-style hat at the airport in Moncton, New Brunswick, in 2002.

∨ The Queen in Ottawa in October 2002.

The Queen's hats have occasionally raised eyebrows—and laughter. She once wore a hat with pheasant feathers to church, a day after being criticized by anti-cruelty groups for wringing the neck of a pheasant that had been injured by a hunter. The choice of hat was a signal, a royal aide said, about her support for such country sports.

In 1991, during a trip to the United States, she was making a speech from a lectern that was much too tall for her, so that all anyone could see was her hat. "I imagine it was her advance man's last day of employment," said one observer.

∨ > Brimless styles were popular with the Queen in the 1970s and 80s. Right: at the Montreal Olympics in 1976. Below: in Moncton, New Brunswick, in 1984.

Fred Chartrand/The Canadian Press

During a 1984 visit to Canada, controversy was raised back in England when Toronto newspapers criticized her appearance. The *Toronto Sun* was particularly scornful of her hats, which it described as "dowdy and matronly." Her defenders said she was a monarch with a real job, not a fashion plate.

One thing never caught on film is the Queen's hat being blown off. Royal milliner Philip Somerville once revealed her secret in a TV documentary: "Every hat has two hatpins, covered in the same material," said Somerville. "I did say to Her Majesty once, 'Well, they're so barbaric.' And she said, 'Yes, Mr. Somerville, but I've never lost a hat.'"

Fred Chartrand/The Canadian Press

< In the 1990s the Queen was often seen in light woven hats with turned-up brims and trim that matched her dress. At Canada Day celebrations in Ottawa in 1997.

> With Prime Minister Brian Mulroney on Parliament Hill at Canada Day 1990.

Ron Poling/The Canadian Press

∧ In a matching coat and hat in Edmonton in 2005.

> The Queen in a turban-style hat—one of her favourite looks—at the unveiling of the Canada Memorial in London in 1994. Prime Minister Jean Chrétien is behind her.

< The Queen in Edmonton in 2005.

∧ Summer look: In bright polka-dots with matching flowers as she ends a visit to Nova Scotia in 1994.

∧ Autumn look: In brown and taupe wool at Vancouver Airport in 2002.

∧ The Queen in Regina in 2005.

∧ Feathers are a common element in the Queen's headgear. Above: she accepts flowers after a tour of the Canadian Light Source Synchrotron in Saskatoon in 2005.

< Arriving in Victoria in 2002.

> On a walkabout at the University of British Columbia in Vancouver in 2002.

∧ In a hat adorned with pheasant feathers at Cambridge in England in 2000. The Queen once wore a hat with pheasant feathers to show her support for the hunting.

∧ Waving goodbye in Ottawa in 1992.

> Royal blue: The Queen on a tour of Sheridan College in Oakville, Ontario, in 2002. She usually wears bright colours on tours so she can be easily seen by the crowds.

CHAPTER 9
ROYAL TOURS FROM BEHIND THE LENS

I t takes an alert and agile photographer with a good eye and quick reflexes to catch a unique and unscripted photo on a royal tour. Some photographers would tell you it also takes dumb luck.

The challenges of covering royal tours have increased through the years. On the early tours, photographers were allowed to move freely, so they could set up shots from interesting angles or catch unscripted moments close-up. Ron Poling, now executive director of picture services for The Canadian Press, recalls the Queen's 1977 visit to Dow's Lake in Ottawa where he was able to get so close to the Queen he almost fell into her when someone accidentally pushed him.

Today, increased security prevents this. "You used to be able to do a walkabout in that you could be walking about also," says photographer Fred Chartrand, who is based in Ottawa. "Now it's all pre-positioning." This means photographers are herded into pens by security officers at least an hour before the Queen or another royal comes by.

< Apparently, it's a car: the Queen and Prince Philip admire an amphibious "penguin" car presented to them in 1964 at Prime Minister Lester Pearson's residence. Pearson's wife, Maryon, is beside the prince and External Affairs Minister Paul Martin is visible over the Queen's shoulder.

Paul Chiasson/The Canadian Press

∧ The Queen appears to get a kick out of an exhibit of former Saskatchewan lieutenant-governors at Government House in Regina in 2005.

"You have to make a decision about where you want to be," says Vancouver-based photographer Chuck Stoody. "There's no following or moving scrum. And you just sort of hope that something happens (from where you are)."

Given these restrictions, luck comes in handy. Stoody recalls a shot he took of Prince Charles and Prince William grinning at each other during their visit to Vancouver, British Columbia in 1998. At the time, a year after Diana's death, Charles had been accused of having a distant relationship with his sons, but this photo certainly suggested otherwise. "I was very lucky to get that picture—it happened in an instant," says Stoody.

∧ A young boy holds his arms out in the hopes of a royal hug from the Queen during a walkabout in Toronto in 1984. He didn't get one.

> Two-year-old Brynn Noble breaks ranks to play as the Queen leaves St. Mary and St. George Anglican Church in Jasper, Alberta, in 2005.

Adrian Wyld/The Canadian Press

< Two women sing an enthusiastic rendition of *God Save the Queen* outside a Victoria cathedral in 2002 while the Queen attends services inside.

ᐯ The Queen tours Sheridan College in Oakville, Ontario, in 2002.

Kevin Frayer/The Canadian Press

Aside from security controls, the Queen can be a tricky subject, says Chartrand. "She's hot and cold. Some days she can radiate in pictures. Other times, it's not there."

Photographing royalty presents another unique challenge thanks to the rules of protocol, says Paul Chiasson, a Montreal-based photographer for The Canadian Press. He and a cameraman once had to wait, with the Queen, for the arrival of a Canadian dignitary who was meeting with her

∧ Nice hat: a well-wisher appears excited to meet the Queen during the monarch's walkabout at Edmonton city hall in 2005.

privately. "We stood there for a good five minutes looking around to all four corners of the room, not able to say a word, as it is bad protocol to address the Queen, while she was standing facing us, obviously getting very impatient, clutching her purse." Not that protocol always rules. Chiasson recalls a formal portrait session where a photographer tried to get the Queen to smile by saying to her, "Show me some teeth." The Queen was not amused.

Chartrand's behind-the-scenes memory of covering the Queen shows a side behind the protocol. It used to be routine for her to hold a media reception at the end of a tour, and he was invited to one on board the royal yacht *Britannia*. The Queen had been briefed on the background of some of the journalists and was told Chartrand had been thrown into an

Tom Hanson/The Canadian Press

∧ It went that-a-way: the Queen and RCMP Commissioner Giuliano Zaccardelli (second from left) appear to be pointing at something off camera as they tour the RCMP musical ride facility in Ottawa in 2002.

< The Queen accepts a bouquet of flowers from a young girl at the RCMP musical ride headquarters in Ottawa in 2002.

Iranian prison in 1981 while covering the American hostage crisis. "She remembered a lot of the briefing," said Chartrand. "She said, 'Oh, Mr. Chartrand, I heard that you spent time in Iran and you were in jail there and it must have caused great concern for your family,'" he recalls. "She stopped and talked about the dreadful situation there. I found that quite candid."

Paul Chiasson/The Canadian Press

^ Royal disappointment: A young boy tries to shake the Queen's hand and then shows his disappointment when she fails to co-operate during a walkabout in Iqaluit in 2002.

^ Lynne Jackson, right, comforts her daughter Mackenzie, 9, as she is overcome with emotion waiting for the Queen to arrive at Sheridan College in Oakville, Ontario, in 2002.

> Five-year-old Sandra Dobler manages to break through police lines at the airport in Kingston, Ontario, to hold hands with the Queen during a 1967 visit.

∧ The Queen walks past a living statue while she tours the Alberta Provincial Museum with museum director Bruce McGillivray in Edmonton in 2005.

< The Queen and Prince Philip are treated to a demonstration of Inuit sports at a school in Iqaluit in 2002.

> She's really a Queen? One young girl appears slightly doubtful during a visit to an elementary school in Sussex, New Brunswick, in 2002.

∧ The Queen and Prince Philip wait for their plane to take off from Regina airport in 2005.

< Not quite her majesty: Conservative Deputy Leader Peter MacKay speaks with actor Scott Thompson, dressed as Queen Elizabeth, during a television spoof outside the House of Commons in 2005.

> The Queen gives one fan a thrill during a walk-about at Old Government House in Fredericton in 2002.

< Is it dead? The Queen seems to give a polar bear rug a wide berth during a visit to the legislature in Yellowknife in 1994.

ʌ Calgarians say so long at the Queen's departure
ceremony at the Saddledome in 2005.

< Const. Kevin Fald (right) of the Edmonton Police Service Historical Unit wears a replica of a 1905 uniform during the Queen's walkabout at Edmonton city hall in 2005.

> The Queen stands in front of a painting of herself in Government House in Regina in 2005.

Paul Chiasson/The Canadian Press

CHAPTER 10

MILESTONES IN A ROYAL LIFE

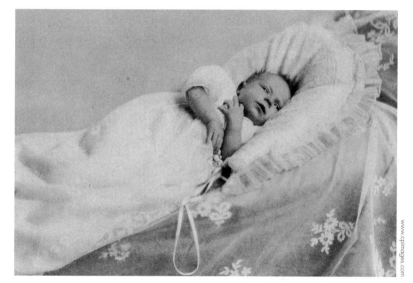

< King George VI and Queen Elizabeth are joined by their daughters, Elizabeth and Margaret, on the balcony of Buckingham Palace on Victory in Europe Day, May 8, 1945.

> One of the earliest known portraits of Queen Elizabeth II, taken when she was a few weeks old in April 1926.

www.cpimages.com

April 21, 1926:
Elizabeth Alexandra Mary is born at her maternal grandparents' home in London.

December 11, 1936:
Her father, George VI, accedes to the throne after the abdication of his brother, Edward VIII.

October 13, 1940:
During an air raid on London, Elizabeth's voice is broadcast for the first time. The 14-year-old princess says British children are "full of cheerfulness and courage" and bearing their share of the "danger and sadness of war."

∧ Princess Elizabeth and her mother at their home in the Piccadilly district of London in July 1936.

∧ Princess Elizabeth and Prince Philip at Buckingham Palace after their wedding on November 20, 1947 at Westminster Cathedral.

April 21, 1944:

Elizabeth turns 18, becomes a counsellor of state, and starts to officially fill in for her father when he is out of the country.

November 20, 1947:

Elizabeth and Philip Mountbatten marry at Westminster Abbey in a ceremony attended by royals and leaders from around the world, and listened to on radio throughout the world.

∧ Princess Elizabeth and Prince Philip wave from the balcony of Buckingham Palace on their wedding day. From left to right, King George VI, Princess Margaret, Lady Mary Cambridge, the bride and bridegroom, Queen Elizabeth and Queen Mary.

November 14, 1948:

Prince Charles is born at Buckingham Palace. The first news reports in Canada mistakenly announce that a girl has been born.

August 15, 1950:

Princess Anne, the Queen's only daughter, is born.

October 2, 1951:

Princess Elizabeth arrives in Quebec City, with the Duke of Edinburgh, for a six-week visit to Canada, her first.

^ The Queen at Buckingham Palace with her maids of honour after her coronation on June 2, 1953.

February 6, 1952:

King George VI dies while Elizabeth is touring Africa.

June 2, 1953:

The Queen's coronation takes place in Westminster Abbey in front of world leaders. It is the first British coronation to be televised.

> The emblems of chivalry are presented during the initial phase of the coronation service. The Queen touches St. George's spurs as the lord great chamberlain kneels before her.

∧ The Queen and U.S. President Dwight Eisenhower at the opening of the St. Lawrence Seaway in St. Lambert, Quebec, in 1959.

< Watched by younger sister Margaret, Princess Elizabeth makes her first radio broadcast from Buckingham Palace on October 12, 1940.

December 25, 1957:

The Queen makes her annual Christmas broadcast on TV for the first time. It is shown throughout the Commonwealth.

June 18, 1959:

The Queen arrives in Canada for her first major tour as ruling monarch. She and the Duke of Edinburgh visit all provinces and territories over six weeks. She officially opens the St. Lawrence Seaway.

www.cpimages.com

< The Queen is dwarfed by a 10-metre-high birthday cake, made of plywood covered with decorations, in front of the Parliament Buildings on July 1, 1967.

∨ The Queen and Prince Andrew walk from the Velodrome to Olympic Stadium at the Montreal Games in 1976.

Wally Hayes/The Canadian Press

February 19, 1960:

The Queen's second son, Andrew, is born, making her the first reigning sovereign to give birth since Queen Victoria.

March 10, 1964:

The Queen's last child, Edward, is born.

Octotober 10, 1964:

A visit by the Queen to Quebec City turns ugly when police crack down on separatist protesters.

January 28, 1965:

The Queen signs the act proclaiming the Maple Leaf as Canada's flag.

Wally Hayes/The Canadian Press

∧ The Queen and her sons (from left to right) Edward, Andrew, and Charles during a tour of the Olympic Games' equestrian facilities in July 1976 at Bromont, Quebec.

July 1, 1967:

The Queen cuts a huge cake in Ottawa to help celebrate Canada's Centennial.

July 1, 1969:

Prince Charles's role as heir to the throne is marked by an investiture ceremony at Caernafon in Wales, watched on television by 200 million people.

July 1976:

The Royal Family gathers in Montreal to watch Princess Anne compete in equestrian events at the Summer Olympics.

Peter Bregg/The Canadian Press

< Dressed in period costume, Prince Charles and
Diana, the Princess of Wales, tour Fort Edmonton
Park in 1983.

June 2, 1977:

The Queen's reign reaches 25 years, setting off celebrations
across Britain and a Commonwealth tour covering almost
90,000 kilometres.

December 30, 1977:

Prime Minister Pierre Trudeau announces that the Queen
has agreed to give up her right to accredit and recall
Canadian diplomats, authorize war declarations, and sign
peace treaties on Canada's behalf.

∧ Prime Minister Pierre Trudeau watches as the Queen signs Canada's constitutional proclamation in Ottawa on April 17, 1982.

October 17, 1980:

The Queen, head of the Church of England, visits Pope John Paul II in the Vatican.

June 13, 1981:

A man shoots several blanks at the Queen as she rides on her horse in a London parade marking her official birthday. She is not injured.

July 29, 1981:

Watched by millions on TV, Prince Charles marries Diana Spencer at St. Paul's Cathedral.

April 17, 1982:

On a rainy day in Ottawa, the Queen signs the act proclaiming Canada's Constitution.

∧ Princes William (left) and Harry wave from a
Toronto balcony in 1991.

June 21, 1982:

The Princess of Wales gives birth to her first child, Prince
William, second in line to the throne.

July 12, 1982:

An intruder breaks into Buckingham Palace, sits on the
Queen's bed and talks to her for 10 minutes before she can
summon help.

October 13, 1986:

The Queen, accompanied by Prince Philip, becomes the first
British monarch to set foot in China.

> Diana, Princess of Wales, attends a park dedication ceremony in Burnaby, B.C., in 1986.

ⅴ Diana glances at photographers during a royal tour stop in Montague, P.E.I., in 1983.

November 20, 1992:
Windsor Castle, one of the Queen's favourite residences, is seriously damaged by fire.

November 26, 1992:
It is announced that the Queen and the Prince of Wales will begin paying tax on their private income.

August 28, 1996:
Prince Charles's marriage to Diana is dissolved.

March 6, 1997:
The Queen unveils the official royal website (www.royal.gov.uk).

August 31, 1997:
Diana is killed in a car accident in Paris. The Queen is criticized for not flying the flag above Buckingham Palace at half-mast, which would have been a break in convention.

May–July 1999:
The Queen opens new national assemblies in Wales and Scotland as power is devolved from the British Parliament.

∧ The Queen Mother, the Queen, and Princess Margaret at Clarence House on the Queen Mother's 100th birthday. Others from left: Prince Andrew, The Countess of Wessex, Prince Charles, Prince Edward (partly hidden), Prince William, an unidentified aide, Peter Phillips, Prince Harry, Prince Philip, and Princess Anne.

August 4, 2000:

The Queen joins her mother on the balcony of Buckingham Palace as tens of thousands of people wish the Queen Mother well on her 100th birthday.

February 9, 2002:

The Queen's only sister, Princess Margaret, dies at age 71.

March 30, 2002:

The Queen Mother dies at age 101.

Chuck Stoody/The Canadian Press

∧ The Queen drops the hockey puck during the ceremonial faceoff between Markus Naslund (right) of the Vancouver Canucks and Mike Ricci of the San Jose Sharks in Vancouver in 2002. Looking on is Ed Jovanovski (left), Cassie Campbell, and Wayne Gretzky.

April 29, 2002:

On the eve of the official start of her Golden Jubilee celebration, the Queen has dinner at 10 Downing Street with Prime Minister Tony Blair and four former British prime ministers who held the position during her reign.

October 6, 2002:

During her Golden Jubilee tour of Canada, the Queen drops the puck at an NHL game in Vancouver.

April 21, 2006:

The Queen celebrates her 80th birthday with a family dinner at Windsor Castle.

∧ The Queen and Prince Philip wave from the top of the stairs as they board their plane to leave Canada in Ottawa in 1997.